CW00850633

Intuitive Writing: Using Writing as a Tool for Discovery and Expression

Tobie Hewitt

My deepest thanks to those who in one way or another encouraged me on this path.

With special thanks to Joy Argento—artist, writer and dear friend—who was one of the first to explore Intuitive Writing and provided input into this book, and to Jill Carlier, whose inquiry about the writing process led to the creation of this book.

. . .

Dedicated to Spirit

Preface

Why are you here? What is your purpose in life? Who are you really? How do you find the answers? When are you going to start living the life you know is inside of you but you can't quite reach?

You are on a journey from a distant place that is as close as your own mind and heart and as far as the beginning of this universe and beyond. You are a spirit joined to the other spirits around you, both here on this physical plane and those on a plane that coexists with ours but at a higher vibrational level. You are here to learn lessons that can only be learned on this physical plane. You know the answers to all of these questions, but, being in a physical body, accessing that information is stymied by all sorts of things: your mood, the environment you are living in, the doctrines or lack thereof that you have been taught as a child, your belief in the non-physical world, the idea that you even have such a plan or that there is any real purpose in life other than being born, living, and dying.

While there are many techniques for getting glimpses of your life plan and purpose, intuitive writing asks you to take control of accessing this information for yourself by using writing as a means to open the communication pathways with both yourself and with the plane of Spirit. It helps you develop your writing so you can both be inspired and informed. And, it provides you with a convenient record of the process so you can continue to learn and grow in order to live your chosen life.

TABLE OF CONTENTS

Introduction

What is Intuitive Writing?

Writing connects you to a variety of levels of awareness and action. It is an organic method of accessing your connections to your deepest core and the widest source of the universe. It connects you to yourself physically, as the act of writing requires some physical action on your part, either by using a writing instrument to mark on paper or tapping out words on a keyboard. It connects you mentally because even when you are channeling the words of others not on your specific plane, your brain processes the input in order to capture it through the act of writing. Emotionally, intuitive writing will help you find that calm, quiet space inside of you for the duration of the time you engage in the activity. And, perhaps most importantly, intuitive writing connects you to your own spirit, which resides within your physical core, to your spirit guides, to the teachers and masters who are ready to help, to all your memories of who you are and the plans you made for your path through this life, and perhaps even others.

Before you were born into this lifetime, you made a plan of how you were going to travel from the beginning to the end, making certain decisions about what lessons you needed to learn and how you were going to do so. Intuitive writing helps you to discern where you are, who you are, maybe who you were in other lifetimes, and how to proceed. Some of this information will come as straightforward guidance, such as actions you can take to move to the next stage on your path and some will be creative and give you ideas for your own writing development. Either way, by using intuitive writing daily, even for five minutes, you can gain a deeper understanding of who you are, your life purpose, and your pathwork. It can also give you a time for meditation and reflection, as writing is an act that involves both mindfulness and awareness.

In this book you will learn the various methods I have used to help writers and non-writers alike access their larger knowledge and creativity by utilizing their intuition. Some methods work for everyone and some work better than others for different individuals. Sometimes the simple suggestion to write without thinking about the writing and to not edit as you do so is enough to start a person down the path of intuitive writing. If you are reading this book, you are already making the commitment to explore this method of accessing your intuitive self and, through that, the vast knowledge available to you through your own spirit and the entire spiritual realm. Intuitive writing will open up a universe of ideas that can help you navigate your path through this life and to create written works that communicate your unique perspective. Every voice is a part of a larger choir, all coming together to acknowledge and continue in the creation of the adventure known as life.

This book is a broader version of the class outline I use when teaching. The idea for this class was sparked when Jill, a woman I met on Facebook, shared her desire to write and yet, at the same time, the difficulty she encountered each time she sat down to do so. I coached her and gave her techniques that would free her ability to capture the words flowing through her head onto paper or in electronic form. The first and most obvious lesson is to write. Just write. Writing is not editing, so you do not need to worry about spelling or grammar or punctuation. The words do not need to be perfect. Right now there is no one grading you and there is no critic who will judge you in any way. When you write, just write. Don't edit. Don't even think. Just allow the words to flow. And do not worry if the flow does not make sense. It is practicing the flow that matters, not the content, as you start on this journey of intuitive writing.

About the Instructor

Who am I? I am a spiritual girl in a physical world. I have recognized the world of Spirit as my true home, and I have recognized that my spirit is currently residing in a physical body in order to learn lessons and share awareness. I have been interacting with and through the Spirit realm as far back in this life as I can remember and serve as an Intuitive Consultant, using various methods and modalities, such as mediumship, psychic awareness, clairvoyance, etc. I am a Reiki II Practitioner and a Crystal Healer. I have been a writer all my life and have employed the techniques I have been given to write all sorts of works, including nine books. I have an MFA in Creative Writing and have taught at the college level, as well as at a local writing center in Rochester, New York, and have helped K-12 students find their poetic voices. I coach writers of different levels, and I am glad to have this opportunity to share what I have learned through writing and teaching with you. I recently coined the title Writing Doula, and in many ways that is what I feel my service is—helping others to give birth to their written works. Part of my practice includes serving as an Intuitive Writing Coach—guiding people to write their own life stories and discover their own path.

In addition to the instruction available through this book, I am available for personal writing coaching. This differs from non-intuitive writing coaching in that I will help you discern the messages you are receiving and offer guidance in helping you interpret and implement this guidance for optimal usefulness in your life. These one-on-one sessions are offered in a variety of manners, from in-person if you are in my area or I am visiting yours, or via telephone or video chats. We will discuss what you wrote, how you feel, and discern possible path choices. I can even contact your spirit guides for additional input.

I hope that you enjoy using this book to learn the intuitive writing techniques and increase your connections to your own spirit and the universe. At the end of this book you can find contact information and other resources to aid you on your journey.

Session 1: Once upon a time . . .

Who are you? Why are you here? What is your path? How do you fulfill your destiny? When will you finally start actualizing your life? This course will help you to use writing to creatively and intuitively access knowledge about yourself, discern your life story, and live the life you are meant to live. Learn to free yourself from expectations, communicate with your own unique spirit, and receive the inspiration the universe has available for you.

Required Supplies: Composition notebook and comfortable writing instrument, or a computer.

The secret to writing is to write. Just . . . start . . . writing. It doesn't matter what you write or if it is any good. Just write the first word you think of or the word for an object in the room and start there. Just like a journey starts with one step, so does a piece of writing start with one word. Now, at this point, you are thinking, "I can't think of anything to write. I have writer's block!" Well, I am here to tell you that writer's block is a myth. Writer's block is nothing more than believing you can't write, so you won't write, so there! It is a tiny tantrum meant to distract you from the task at hand, which is to write. Now, refusing to give in to the myth does not mean you will write beautiful prose every time you sit down to write. I am writing this book as a draft, and I can write anything I want. I do not expect it to be perfect. That desire for instant perfection is at the root of "writer's block." Instantaneous writing is not meant to be perfect. In fact, YOU are not meant to be perfect! You are meant to be experiencing this physical life and all the messy and interestingly imperfect parts of it, which in this case means writing. When you started walking, it was not a pretty thing to witness. You got one foot placed and then you fell. You stood, you fell. You slightly lifted one foot to take a step, you fell. Over and over again until you learned the muscle memory necessary to actually walk. Even today, you may not be as graceful as a ballerina as you traverse the path of your life, but you can manage to get from one spot to another without falling over. This need to practice what is new to you applies to writing as well. The payoff here is that not only are you about to learn to write without fear and trepidation, but you are going to learn how to access your own intuitive gifts in order to discern your path through this life.

Now, all writing is, in a sense, an act of discovery, about self or the world or a thought. Intuitive writing takes writing one step beyond because through practice you will begin to request information from spirits, guides, teachers, and masters. You will begin to discern when you are gaining information, when you are gaining guidance, and when you are actually gaining wisdom. It is fun to try to discern these subtle differences, and my students often ask how they can tell the difference between their own voice and that of other beings and my answer is always the same—it really doesn't matter! By that I mean that it doesn't matter if when you are writing you think you are just being creative and writing down your own intrinsic thoughts or if you are getting wisdom from one of the masters. Since you are a spirit, connected to all other spirits, and to the oneness of the universe through the interdependent web, everything you do is a spirit-informed act. Even when you think you are just being creative, subtle input from spirit, yours and others', enters into everything you write. As we continue, you will begin to sense when these bits of information begin to enter into your writing and recognize the guidance you are receiving. So . . . let's start writing! Here is an easy exercise you can do without causing yourself any undue stress:

Tell yourself you will write for only five minutes and use a timer. First, you need to center yourself. Take a few deep and slow breaths. Think of allowing air to enter your nose and flow gently down through your chest and into your belly and then release the air gently through your mouth. Do this several times. As you do this, concentrate on your breaths and try not to think about anything other than the air entering and leaving your body. After a minute or so you should begin to feel more calm and focused than when you started. Start the timer and then . . . write for five minutes (in a composition notebook or on the computer) . . . without stopping or editing. When the timer goes off, you MUST stop. And DO NOT READ WHAT YOU WROTE. Walk away! Do this every day for a week. Then, you may read what you wrote, but you may not edit it. The next week, add a minute (or two or five) and do the same thing. After a couple of weeks, your body and mind will ache for those short moments of expression. After a month, you may edit if you wish, or simply keep the writing as is and keep on going.

This exercise is called free writing or stream-of-consciousness writing. You start with no specific idea in mind but simply allow the words to fall through you into written form. It takes a little practice because you need to silence the internal editor, which is always trying to insert its two cents in about word choice or idea or whatever it feels at any given moment is below its expectations as it strives for perfection (which is something to aim for, not necessarily to achieve). Practicing stream-of-consciousness writing allows you to free the writer within and to create a useful pathway through which intuitive knowledge can flow without impediment. It is a fine method to learn to free yourself from that incessant editor.

I have been asked whether automatic writing and intuitive

writing, especially in terms of stream-of-consciousness writing, are the same thing. Automatic writing is different from intuitive writing. In the former the writer is not aware of what is being written while in the latter there is this awareness. It is believed that automatic writing is a form of communication from a spirit through an incarnate person who enters into a form of trance and allows the spirit to take control of the writing function, essentially bypassing the physical brain of the person. While this is a form of spirit communication, I believe it to be an arduous one in terms of the relinquishment of control by the incarnate being. I prefer to allow spirit to work with me, rather than through me, which is pretty much how this paragraph was written. In fact, working together, those in spirit and I have worked on numerous books and other written pieces. Sometimes, I admit I am not fully aware of what is being written until later when I read the piece for editing. It is a process that allows for input and guidance from spirit while addressing a topic of my choice (most of the time).

Asking a question in writing

In order to start communicating with your spirit, other spirits, guides, teachers, and masters, you should begin a routine of asking questions of these beings. It is easier to ask questions and receive answers than to just wait for one of these entities to communicate with you, especially if you are not familiar with communicating with them. It is best to start with simple questions, like the name of your spirit guide, than, say, what the meaning of life is.

Center yourself and then write down or type a question. It should be short and not require a complicated answer. In the future, you can ask questions that require more involved answers, but for now, let's keep it simple. If you do not know the name of your spirit guide, for example, you could write, "What is the name of my spirit guide?" That simple! Then, write down the very next thing that pops into your head, even if it seems strange. It could be a name you know, such as that of a loved one who has passed over, or it could be a name you do not knowingly have a connection to. The important thing is to not allow the internal editor to alter any words that you sense. Just write them down. As time goes on, and you feel more comfortable, you can seek out loved ones on the other side and engage them in conversation through writing. It is possible to gain insight into their lives and your family history and even guidance. You can access teachers and masters and get more philosophically fulfilling answers to questions you have. Sometimes the answers will make no sense in the moment, but when you go back and read the answers over time, the content may start to become more meaningful to you.

How do you recognize valid communication versus making it up? At this point in your process of becoming familiar with the practice of intuitive writing it is often difficult to feel the difference, but with practice and time you will be able to discern a subtle shift when you are receiving from the Spirit realm. This shift in perception is very real, and also very small. It involves allowing your spirit senses to work instead of your physical senses. When I write I can feel this slight shift in awareness. For example, I will think, "What next?" and then wait to receive the input from spirit that guides a great deal of my writing. It is not difficult, but it takes practice.

To explain further, you are composed of two bodies. One is physical and the other is a spirit, which resides within your physical body but can extend itself outside of this body as your aura and can even leave the body, while still connected through a thin silver cord that attaches at your solar plexus chakra (a topic for further exploration in a future book). Your physical body has five senses through which it receives impressions from the physical world that help you to navigate this existence. The spirit body has six (or more) senses that have the same functions as the physically based ones, but these perceive ethereal input from the other side or from metaphysical aspects of this side. For example, one can perceive the energies of a flower or a vista that are not available to the physical senses. It is this spirit body's senses that allow for communication with spirits who do not have corporeal bodies. You can hear their words, or detect a familiar scent associated with a loved one with the senses of hearing and smell based in the spirit body, which are then transformed as signals to your physical senses so it seems as though it was your physical body all along that was sensing these perceptions. You also use the sixth sense of intuition to guide you through impressions of the world around you and, for that matter, to help you as you intuitively write.

I have been asked how to recognize whether the communication from spirit is valid or if it is being made up. At first, this is a difficult distinction to make, especially when the communication is hard to believe, i.e., seemingly strange. This is where trust in the process comes in. While it is fine to believe that you are making up the answers to your questions, how can you be sure that you are? And why does it matter? I know, that seems like a strange question, but your ability to give validity to the writing is really not important at this point. What is important is that you are practicing writing and that you are asking for information to be given to you through your intuition, which is part of this process—you are trying to open up that communication pathway with spirit. After a while, hopefully a brief while, you will recognize that you are writing valid information of which you have no knowledge, i.e., that the words you are writing do not fall neatly into your regular thoughts or writing patterns. This recognition that the words and ideas are coming from an external source is a primary purpose of intuitive writing.

Why is it okay to make it up, although you really aren't? In my Intuitive Writing Workshop, we discussed whether what they were writing was true or fiction (i.e., were they receiving messages from spirit or making it up in their heads) and I told them it didn't matter. Why? Because the exercises in intuitive writing are for both your creative self and for communicating with your higher self, which may, indeed, be one and the same thing! Often, when we write or create art of some sort we say we are inspired. What does that mean? To inspire means to breathe in, which could be air or ideas, but it also means to be guided by an external source, as in to be divinely inspired or to be moved by the input of another, such as an inspiring idea that moves us to action. So when we write, we are often inspired to do so and whether it seems to us to come organically from within our brains or from another source, it is most likely coming from a space that is not located in our physical brain but, rather, from our spirit or other spiritual origins.

When you make something up, then, you really are not able to distinguish the origins until you have practiced enough to do so, to perceive where the idea or the next word is coming from. When I pause for a moment and allow the words to flow through me without impediment, I often find that they have a certain color to them that I recognize comes from spirit, either my own or from others. How do we know how we are perceiving and does it matter whether we believe it is somehow just us (rarely) or some external source? If our purpose is to improve our writing and to use it for communicating with spiritual sources, then acknowledging the source allows for gratitude to be a part of the process, to be thankful to the beings for the kindness in helping us and inspiring us as we capture the words floating through our brains and down our arms to our fingers.

It is a subtle shift in the perceptions between the physical senses and the senses of the spirit and is so subtle most people don't perceive the difference, but once you have trained yourself through the exercises in intuitive writing you have a better chance of being able to discern when spirit is communicating with you. Intuitive writing is a series of techniques meant to inform and enrich your life—creatively and spiritually. It is meant to free your voice and your awareness to capture the flow of ideas and information that is available to you at any time.

One of the most important questions you may have already asked through this instruction is "Who is my spirit guide?" This is important because communication with this spirit is a vital aspect of your growth as a writer and as a spirit. If you have not done so, please write this question down and receive the answer. Spirit guides help us in many ways, both by sharing information we need and also being a welcome friend. My spirit guide, Roger, has been with me for as long as I can remember. We shared a lifetime together in Dover, England, in the 1800s. We were, at that time as we are now, involved in paranormal and metaphysical research. We decided that we would work together at this time with me incarnate and him on the spirit plane. He is a very dear person and very helpful in my daily life and also when we sit down to write, such as right now.

Spirit guides can help us enter into pleasant and interesting moments and also help us avoid rather unpleasant and questionable moments. They can provide us with information we need and inspire us to pursue projects. Unlike us, who, for the most part, cannot remember all the details of the lives we have planned, the paths we need to follow to fulfill our goals, and past life information that may be pertinent, our guides are able to more easily access this information and share it with us at appropriate times. Knowing your guide's name helps communication because there is nothing so rude as simply saying "Hey you, could you help me a bit?" It is much more pleasant to develop a rapport with this person since they are part of your life from beginning to end. In the next section, your guide will help as you write the story of your life, so having their name will more easily allow you to communicate with them.

It is best to start your journey by following the exercises in this section: center yourself, practice stream-of-consciousness writing for a minimum of five minutes a day, do not edit what you write, write down questions for spirit, and then write down the first answer that comes through your mind. Over time you will notice that not only are you writing more freely, but that there is an intelligence in the questioning and answering exercise that seeks to inform you. And accessing this ability is the basis for intuitive writing.

Session 2: Write the story of your life going forward, looking back!

Awareness of the larger aspects of your life is a foundational aspect of intuitive writing. Now that you have practiced the techniques in Session 1 for some time and become comfortable with them, write your life story before it happens — manifest that vision of you! Everyone has a story to tell. It may not be true, or it could be, or maybe not. But, everyone has a story. You are going to tell the story of your life going forward.

I have re-read this first paragraph of this section and I can see where there may be some confusion about time and space, so let's deal with this before we move into the exercise. To begin with, all space is here and all time is now. There are schools of modern physics that support this, but I am a writer and mystic, not a scientist, so for those who wish to expand their knowledge base, I recommend *The Tao of Physics* by Fritjof Capra.

Because of the nature of the universe, everything can potentially be accessed at any time in any space. For this exercise, that means that intuitive writing can help you access the plan for this current life. Where did this plan come from and why? You wrote it before you were born during the time between incarnations (you didn't seriously believe that a book about intuitive writing would stick to writing and not delve into the workings discovered by mysticism, did you?).

Here is a brief summary of existence. You are a spirit connected to other spirits through what is known as the interdependent web of existence, which was created by a larger being I like to call the Creative Spirit in order to remove any tint of dogma from the explanation (and because that is the name spirit gave me to use). In reality, in this physical world we are all one, differentiated into separate bodies and the lesson of that is that we are, because of this illusion of separateness, supposed to learn about each other as we exist on earth and also how to interact in a peaceful and loving manner. We are still working on that series of lessons.

As individual spirits within the larger framework of the interdependent web, we are currently in the phase of a cycle of incarnating on Earth. That means we inhabit a shell we refer to as our physical body, with all its benefits and challenges to learn from on this particular path. We transition between the physical and spiritual planes. We have decided to call this "death" but I think that is too final a word since it is simply entering a respite between physical lives.

During this respite, this stay on the spiritual plane, we enjoy the immediate company of loved ones who have transitioned before us, and we work out a plan for the next incarnation. This plan can be very precise, moving from moment to moment, but usually it is a bit freer than that, creating touchpoints, moments we need to reach and learn from before we move on to the next one and so on until we return to the spirit plane. We can certainly change the plan at any time, either on the spirit plane or after we incarnate, but the lessons that needed to be learned still need to be learned, so either we need to return again for that particular set of lessons or we change course a bit while incarnate and create a new situation to learn from.

One of the purposes of intuitive writing, in addition to accessing inspiration for creative expression or communicating with our loved ones in spirit, is to discover our life plan. When we start to seek the basis for our lives during this incarnation, we can look back to the time we created the plan for this life and we can look forward to the moments we need to reach. We can also, because of the nature of the illusion of time, project ourselves into the future to write the story of our lives looking backward. All of these viewpoints enter into an understanding of our goals and purpose of being here.

You can start writing this story any time during this exploration of intuitive writing, but I would recommend becoming comfortable with the techniques you have been practicing in Session 1 before you delve into writing your life story.

Each writing session should start with becoming centered by taking a few deep breaths and then non-stop freewriting for five minutes. This helps to free yourself from your normal daily mindset and allow you to enter into the space of discovery available during intuitive writing. You could even extend this warm-up session to ten or fifteen minutes if you like. Once you are centered and feeling free and comfortable, reach out in writing to your guide for help. "Roger, help me please" is often enough to ask my guide to focus on the task at hand. Your guide's help is important because they retain and remember the life plan you created before this lifetime. The two of you, and possibly others, sat down and wrote out this plan and you gave it to your guide for safekeeping.

Now, stop writing for a few moments and ask yourself, "What do I want my life to be?" Think of what your best life would be: your career, your environment, your relationships, etc. Use your senses to create these as fully as possible. What does it feel like to sit at your desk in your dream job? Where do you drink your morning coffee in your perfect home? Imagine looking into the eyes of your life partner and describe what you see. Once you have this life clearly in mind or even just hints, start writing down every detail you can think of to include. Write it as though you are writing at some future point in time and looking back, as though it has already happened. This point of view creates a level of intent. It creates in the universe a path backward to the moment you are in. For example, my life plan included writing books that would help people to discern their spirit and their life plan while creating a comfortable space to learn some of the basic functioning of the universe. I wrote that last sentence while allowing my spirit/higher self/guide space to place each word in a way that would trigger a memory that this was one of my life goals. (As a side note, when I veer off course, which I do sometimes, I am always drawn back to writing to find the answers to the question "What next?")

Be creative. Allow inspiration to flow through you. Let your guide take the reins and fill you with words. Relinquish control to the universal flow and see if there are any details floating around pertaining to you. Are you making this up? Is this real or imagined? Does it matter? Even the greatest acts of imagination have their bases in a spiritual awareness and knowledge. These are being created in conjunction with a much larger plan than the one we can discern at this time. The Creative Spirit, too, has a plan or set of plans for the universe it created and sometimes we are able to discern a wisp of that plan in our lives. Writing it down makes it real for us and the more reality we can stand on, even though it has a tendency to shift at the most interesting times, the more focused we can remain on the tasks at hand. Remember, it's not all work and no play. If you envision a month in Hawaii at some point during this lifetime, write it down. This exercise both helps you remember and helps you set the intent for the touchpoints of your life. Write the story of your life.

I suggest you pursue this activity over the course of a week or two or more. You can use some of the writing suggestions in Session 3 to help keep your writing flowing. In addition, you are invited to check the end of this book for information about contacting me for individual writing/intuitive coaching and consulting.

Continue writing for guidance (10 minutes per day) and refine your best life scenario.

Session 3: Techniques for setting intent and actualizing your life story

Congratulations! By now, if you have been following and implementing intuitive writing, you have started to use the practices as ways of accessing your intuitive sense and found information and guidance for living a more guided and fulfilling life. If you have not done so already, please go back to the first week of writing, during which you mostly practiced stream-of-consciousness writing, and read what you wrote. Do you see patterns? Are you able to discern ideas that may not synch up with your usual way of thinking? Do these ideas feel as though they are guiding you? As you read do you find that there is an awareness growing of influences external to yourself? Have you made the acquaintance of your spirit guide and turned to that person for help and guidance? Your life is a journey and only you can decide at any given time if you are going to continue on the straight path or turn right or left to follow a different story line. BUT! The interesting aspect about this supposed decision is: Is it different from the life plan you originally created? Are you really changing the direction, or did a series of events push you onto or further onto the path you had chosen?

Sometimes, when it seems as though everything is going wrong or your every step is countered by what appears to be failure, it is in fact guidance that what you are doing is not actually what you had planned and the supposed "failures" are merely course corrections to get you back on the correct path through this life for optimal growth and service to others, which is also part of being here. An example of this in my life is that I decided it might be nice to offer classes at a local metaphysical shop on paranormal topics. Each time I offered a class, only one or two people would express interest. I decided after listening to the guidance being offered to me from spirit and from friends who have a like understanding of pathwork, that it would be better to spend the time I would have invested in the classes writing a series of Kindle books so that more people could learn the lessons at their leisure and for less money. As I write this, I can feel that comforting vibration of recognizing this is the path to take. Because I am a writer and mystic, I often find, as I write, that the words are as much for me as these are for my readers. Writing is a way of recording the guidance so that it can be acknowledged and incorporated into a life path.

Update: I decided, because of the continued interest of a few dedicated students to continue teaching these small classes. Benefitting two or three people who will then share this knowledge with others is worth the time investment. In return, these people have encouraged me to start a podcast, which is on my short to-do list! Stay tuned!

So, how do you take the writing you have been doing and start to use it productively in your life and how, should you face a hesitation in your writing, do you continue writing and discerning the guidance you seek?

First of all, you should keep asking your guides for help, in writing! Notice that I wrote guides in plural. Yes, you have a spirit guide who is with you from birth throughout your life and who you will have a chance to thank face to face at a later date. But you also have loved ones from whom you can seek guidance. You can write to your father, for example, and ask him a question. Write down the first thing that comes to mind and create a conversation back and forth between the two of you, writing down both sides of the dialogue. If the answers do not at first make sense to you, keep working on building this new aspect of your relationship. After a while, the answers will take on relevance. Try this with various loved ones on the other side.

In addition to your primary spirit guide, you will, over time, realize that there are others who are there to guide you and even inspire you. I have always been aware of a healing spirit who has, until recently, been in the background, waiting for the time to step forward. Her name is Nakoma and she is Native American from the Southwest. She has become more prominent in my life since I pursued training in Reiki and Crystal Healing. We are now preparing to create a healing modality that incorporates intuitive consulting as well as energetic healing during a session.

There are also teachers and masters you can reach out to for deeper guidance and knowledge. These are primarily beings who have not incarnated on Earth but, instead, live on other planes of existence and serve to provide higher knowledge for us. You should feel free, for example to write to an archangel you feel drawn to, such as Michael. Rest assured that he or she will answer your questions. This knowledge often has to do with a different level of understanding of broader information, such as how to work toward peace or to live a more loving life or how to work more fully for the betterment of those around us. This still qualifies as life-path guidance, because if you are drawn to communicate with these beings, it is a sure sign that you are here, at least in part, to help the larger community. Practicing intuitive writing can not only help you to live the life you planned to live, but it can also help to remind you of the aspects of service you had set intent to accomplish before your current incarnation. In the details and demands of our daily lives, we can lose the larger purpose of our lives. Connecting to teachers, masters, and archangels can help to remind us of our greater purpose.

Perhaps you would like a more visual way to delve into the guidance you are receiving. Here are some useful methods that you can use to bring in a more visual aspect to your awareness.

On a large sheet of paper or poster board, create a visual representation of your intent, with your goal in the middle and the steps to achieving that goal radiating out from there. You can go through your writing and pull out words, ideas, and phrases that help you design this map of your path and the steps needed to reach your goal. You can create several paths, perhaps all based on the same or similar ideas and goals and consider which path might be worth pursuing for the time being. Because you are the creator of your life plan and, therefore, of your life, feel free to put anything in the map that may occur to you. You can even use different colors for different aspects of the map. For example, you could put ideas for specific actions in one color and ideas for further thought or inspiration in another color. You could create the map as a series of spirals rather than straight lines, so that certain points intersect visually. The purpose of this exercise, which you can do over and over again to see how things change, is to complement your intuitive writing by creating a visual representation of the ideas that you have been exploring while writing. It is a way to bring further focus and, I hope, answers to your questions about who you are, why you are here at this time, and how to move forward in an optimal manner to live your best life.

Another way to visually focus on your intuitive gleanings is to create a vision board. Get an appropriate-sized poster board and paste pictures cut from magazines that portray aspects of your life goals onto it. Again, you can look through your writing to see if there are any words, ideas, or phrases that seem to repeat more than others and then try to find visual representations to place on your board. Or you could do a search for the word on the internet and select images associated with that word, etc. You can select not only pictures, but also words that inspire or challenge you. Feel free to add to the board whenever you are moved to do so. It, like your life, is a work in process! Place this where you can see it frequently to remind you of the life you are actualizing. You can even use it as a focal point for meditation. Using it as such might invite other ideas to arise that will answer more of your questions or give you inspiration or create a hunger to explore more deeply certain aspects of discovery.

Now, let's move on to exercises that will help you to actualize your goals, or take steps to your daily or life goals. The intuitive writing that you have been doing has connected you to your own spirit and to the world of spirit around you. By now, you should be aware that you are not in this alone and that there are plenty of beings willing and able to help you live your optimal life. Here are some steps you can take to actualize, i.e., bring into your sphere of reality, your goals.

Create an affirmation or affirmations and repeat these daily and often! Select a goal you would like to work toward and write it down on an index card and keep it with you at all times (laminate it if you like). Write it as though it already exists, as though it has already been achieved. Read it often and say it out loud. For example, "I am living a life that serves others and provides income for myself." Be as specific as you can be and feel the ideas resonate within you. If they do not feel correct, change them. Go back over your writing and look for phrases that more closely align with your desires. When you find an idea that resonates, you will feel a certain tingle up your spine or a sense of knowing that is unmistakable and that is the idea you should concentrate on in this time.

You can also use visualization: as often as you are able, sit quietly and visualize the life you are trying to manifest. Use your imagination to allow your five senses to engage with the environment that this life will take place in. See yourself engaging in the actions in the environment you want to be in. Close your eyes and imagine what the place looks like or what smells are wafting around you. See with the eyes of your heart the details of the space and how it feels to be there. Move around in this visualization (while sitting still) and allow yourself to feel fully immersed in the action. For example, if your goal is to work outdoors in a nature setting building things, then consider every aspect of this as you practice visualization. Feel the breeze, smell the flowers, touch the tools you are using, see the lush land around you, hear the sound of the birds in the trees surrounding the spot in which you are working. In your mind, make it as real as you can. If a challenge to this visualization should crop up, like how are you earning a living, let the visualization begin to guide you toward a solution. Over time, if this is truly your goal, your visualization will move closer and closer to actualizing.

In creating the life you wish to live, or that you discovered through intuitive writing, you can go one step further and make another copy of the goal, place it under a crystal, light a white candle, and meditate on actualizing the goal, again in the present tense. Clear quartz crystals are best for this exercise because these are considered an all-purpose crystal. Make sure to cleanse the crystal by briefly running cold water over it. You do not want other vibrations not associated with you and your desires to influence this activity. You can also cleanse a crystal by placing it in a window so that the full moon energies can cleanse it. A few days of these vibrations and the crystal is as good as new. You do not have to spend hours and hours doing this. Once you have set your intention for a few days, the crystal will hold that intention and send energies into the goal under it.

Another way to boost your intentions and create the life you have envisioned is to build a crystal grid and activate it during the new moon. The new moon is the time to mobilize energies to bring new ideas, actions, and dreams into your life and crystal grids help to let the universe know that you are ready to receive the changes that are waiting for you. They fortify and renew your commitment to your life path and allow you to have an energy source working to give reality to that commitment.

A crystal grid can be large and complicated or very simple. Most grids are based on a series of circles surrounding a center stone or object you find empowering. My current grid is on the small side and contains clear quartz crystals, rose quartz, and malachite and has been activated and running for several months. I activated it by using a crystal point to join the crystals' energies together by moving the point over the other crystals in a manner of connecting them. During this I say, "And it harm none, so mote it be," as I connect one crystal to the other by drawing an "imaginary" line in the air above it to the next crystal in the pattern. You can also say something like, "this or something better," or even, "make it so." After you have connected the crystals energetically in the grid pattern, you can place the connector crystal in the center, point up, and spend a few moments contemplating the goal(s) you are working on. The energies will continue to pulse for as long as the grid is allowed to run, usually until the next full moon, during which one releases the ideas, dreams, and goals into the universe. (You draw these toward you during the new moon and release them during the full moon.) My current grid has been running because its purpose is ongoing. One of the goals it is supporting is writing this book! While the grid is activated, you can stand or sit in front of it and send intention into the grid. Just like intuitive writing itself, or the vision board, or affirmations, the grid serves as a reminder of who you are and the path you wish to follow through your life. It helps to make the long path into shorter steps, if you wish, by focusing more narrowly on some aspect of your goal.

You can set the grid during the new moon and dismantle it during the full moon and place the crystals used where the light of the full moon can cleanse their energies so that they are fresh for the next time you use them. Clear quartz is an all around good crystal to use, while different colored crystals have different uses. Rose quartz and malachite, or any pink or green crystals, are heart chakra stones and provide energies for healing, love, and abundance. I will be writing a more detailed book about chakras, crystals, and grids soon.

Now, you may be wondering if this isn't a bit too "mystical" for you, but by now you have contacted and communicated with your own spirit, your spirit guide, and all sorts of spirit plane beings for information and guidance. You have created mind maps and vision boards, and you have even created what could be called a mini grid when you used the single crystal, a written copy of your goal, and a candle to focus your energies on your path. Using crystals is simply one more way of working with the universe to strengthen your resolve to work toward your goals. Working with crystals can lend a physical manifestation to your spiritual work. Placing a copy of your goal affirmation in the center of the grid, under the clear crystal point, helps to flow energy continuously into that idea. When you dismantle your grid, the energies that have been continuously flowing through it are further dispersed through the universe and increase the power of your intention.

This is a good moment to say a few words about worry and fear. It is said that worrying is praying for the thing you do not want to happen to happen. Worry and fear act against actualizing your goals and energies. I know it is hard sometimes to release worry and fear but with practice it can be done. Franklin D. Roosevelt said, "The only thing we have to fear is fear itself." Fear and worry are negative energies that counteract the powerful positive energies we strive to work with. Staying in the positive realm allows us to freely work toward activating the goals we wish to achieve. When we give into fear and worry, we waste the energy we could otherwise be putting to good use. From the moment you sat down to begin writing intuitively and through the exercises in this book, you may have worried that you might draw in negative energies. This would be impossible as by the open aspect of taking charge of your life you were acting in and of the light that binds our spirits all together into oneness. The loving support of the interdependent web also helps to ward off negative energies, so, in truth, we are always surrounded by healing, peace, light, and love, and nothing we do in this frame of mind and with an open and loving heart can bring negative energies into our lives. Even when an event occurs that we perceive as negative, we can rest assured that it is but a learning moment and that in the end there will be a positive outcome. Our perceptions while incarnate are narrow for a reason, so we can learn from specific events and actions. When we engage in intuitive writing and other mind-opening modalities, we are telling the universe we are ready for increased knowledge. This would be a part of our life plan. In truth, that you were drawn to this learning experience means you had planned at some point in your life to avail yourself of a broader view of your life and the world around you. Intuitive writing and the exercises it entails bring you into alignment with your deepest and truest knowledge.

Sometimes writing appears to be more difficult than others. It is not that it is necessarily harder to do, but when it flows less easily than what you are used to it is time to try other methods to trigger the writing. Walking away for a few moments is a good first step to overcoming these moments. If you are able to, go outside and breathe the air and look around you and really feel the world around you. Notice the small details. Really feel yourself as a part of this environment. If you cannot go outside, walk around your living space and pay attention to every detail. Try to look at the space as a visitor would. What captures your interest? Is something asking you to write about it? What can you discover about your environment, either inside or outside, that serves to inform your state of being at this moment? Contemplating in this manner can give you a deeper appreciation of and insight into the world around you, of which you are and always have been an integral part. Return to your notebook or computer and write what you discovered and what you learned from it. This, too, is intuitive writing, but allows you to take a more active role in the process.

How else can you invite words to flow? Here are some other ideas for you to try.

Select a book from your shelves and hold it closed in your hands. Close your eyes and ask for general guidance or you can even ask a more specific question. Keep your eyes closed and open the book to a random page and place your finger on the open page. Yes, you might end on something less inspiring, like "the." In this case, look at the words around that one and see if any seem to vibrate toward you. It may take a couple of tries, but you will find that there is a kernel of truth leaping out at you and asking to be explored in writing.

If you have a tarot or oracle deck (you may want to get one or two as you go forward with your new path), you can take the cards in your hands, ask for guidance, shuffle the cards, and select one or two from the deck. Really look at the images on the cards. What are they saying to you? What ideas are arising in your mind? These are the things you should now write about to further explore their guidance.

Go to a metaphysical shop and explore the crystals there. While I always recommend a clear quartz crystal, you may be drawn to something else. Or perhaps there are several that speak to you (this would be a good time to select stones for your grid work). Be sure to cleanse these in full moon light or under cold water (check first that your crystal(s) can survive being in water). When you sit down to write, you can try holding one (or more) of the crystals in your hands and allow the energies to help you get started. Pay close attention to discern if the crystal is giving you useful knowledge. Crystals are very old beings and contain information from over a very long time span.

Intuitive writing is a mode of communication with spirit in which you are an active participant. Through your writing and its subsequent interaction with spirit, you gain knowledge, guidance, and insight about your purpose and path in this life. It is both informative and creative. As you continue working in this modality of communication, you will find that you are not alone in the universe but instead have many loved ones and guides in spirit who are all eager to help you to grow through this incarnation. It does, however, require that you work to gain this knowledge. You simply must sit down and write in order to discover the words and their meanings that will lead you to a more fulfilling life. I would like to share a passive modality of guidance that asks only that you stay aware and that is the highly comforting and informative aspects of synchronicity.

First, get a small notebook or create a space on your phone to take and keep notes. Every time you see and/or hear or think or say the same word in two different ways at the same time, write it in your little book and note the date and time. For example, recently I was reading something on the internet and at the same time I was listening to the television. At the exact same moment I read the word "create" I heard it being said by someone on the show I was listening to. Of course I recorded this, what I call, synch moment, as I have been doing for several years. Sometimes the words do not seem to have any discernable meaning at the time of the synch. At those moments, though, I recognize that synchronicity is a way for the universe to let me know it is watching. It is an acknowledgement that I am living my best life and doing the best I can in that moment. It is a pat on the back from spirit.

On the other hand, it is interesting to see if a message becomes clear. Over time, the words may start to form ideas or even come together to offer words of encouragement. The message may take a little thought to discern, but it will definitely be there. For me to receive the word "create" in addition to the other synchs I have received not only is a sign of approval, but also an encouragement to continue creating! Because I have dedicated this incarnation to serving spirit, I have kept myself open to all sorts of signs from them about my life and pathwork. Even working on this book has been a collaborative project between spirit and me! Synchronicity is another mode that spirit uses to communicate with those of us who are incarnate!

Just when you think you have all things in your control, and that you are able to follow your path and you know what it is, and you can talk to guides and you are getting a real good vibe all the time, then I need to tell you that you have free will to change anything. So then we get to the whole issue of free will and the fact of the matter is that at any time you can stop what you are doing and do something else. You can literally take a right turn even though you got the feeling you should take a left or vice versa and the point of the matter is yes you have free will to change anything and even everything but, quite honestly, how do you know whether the thing you are changing to is actually a part of your path or not. So the best thing you can do is to try to live your best life, to determine information from the other side through intuitive writing, and to find your way through your life on this planet on this plane and not worry whether you are doing the absolute right thing or the wrong thing but that you are just continuing to exist, enjoy, and live in bliss. As Joseph Campbell recommended, "follow your bliss," and that is the main point of it all—to gather as much guidance through your intuitive writing and follow your own sense of bliss and to live your life in a manner that does no harm and, instead, lifts you and your fellow creatures to a higher vision of life.

I hope that you enjoy using this book to learn the intuitive writing techniques and increase your connections to your own spirit and the universe. In addition to the instruction available through this book, I am available for personal writing coaching. This differs from non-intuitive writing coaching in that I will help you discern the messages you are receiving and offer guidance in helping you interpret and implement this guidance for optimal usefulness in your life. These one-on-one sessions are offered in a variety of manners from in-person if you are in my area or I am visiting yours, or via telephone or video chats. We will discuss what you wrote, how you feel, and discern possible path choices. I will also be able to contact your spirit guides for additional input.

Please contact me through my website, www.tobiehewitt.com. You may write me a message or call or text me at (585) 755-9922. I will be adding podcasts and online classes soon. Please join my mailing list at my website to be notified of these new opportunities. I also have a Facebook page, www.facebook.com/TobieHewitt.IntuitiveConsultant/, where you may leave me a message and learn of other offerings.

About the Author

Tobie Hewitt is a former English professor, an accomplished wordsmith, a seasoned motivational speaker/teacher, and an Intuitive Life Coach/Consultant. She currently has seven books listed on Amazon.com, including *Simple Gifts: Living a Spirited Life*, which shares what it is like to be a spiritual girl in a physical world. She has helped countless individuals find their writing voice and connection to the wider sphere in which they live. Please visit her website, www.tobiehewitt.com. You may contact her at thewitt3@gmail.com or (585) 755-9922 to schedule a presentation or an individual consultation.

Printed in Great Britain
by Amazon

39559852R00025